FRANCE 2016 HUMAN RIGHTS REPORT

EXECUTIVE SUMMARY

France is a multiparty constitutional democracy. The president of the republic is elected by popular vote for a five-year term. Voters elected Francois Hollande to that position in 2012. The upper house (Senate) of the bicameral parliament is elected indirectly through an electoral college, while the public elects the lower house (National Assembly) directly. The 2012 presidential and National Assembly elections, the 2014 elections for the Senate, and the 2015 regional elections were considered free and fair.

Civilian authorities maintained effective control over the security forces.

In November 2015 President Hollande declared a nationwide state of emergency following terrorist attacks in Paris and Saint-Denis. The parliament subsequently extended the state of emergency five times. Following the July terrorist attack in Nice, it was extended to the middle of July 2017. The state of emergency gives significantly expanded powers to police and state authorities. Prefects in all regions may prohibit public demonstrations or gatherings and close provisionally concert halls, restaurants, or any public place. Police and prefects also may search homes without a warrant and authorities may place persons of interest and their relatives under house arrest if they are deemed to pose a threat to national security. United Nations human rights experts, some nongovernmental organizations (NGOs), and Green Party members of parliament expressed concern the state of emergency negatively affected the balance between security and individual rights, but it enjoyed widespread legislative and public support throughout the year.

The most significant human rights problems during the year included a number of anti-Semitic and anti-Muslim incidents, although incidents decreased substantially in comparison to 2015. Government evictions of Roma from illegal camps were also reported. Lengthy pretrial detention remained a problem.

Other reported human rights problems included instances of excessive police use of force against detainees at time of arrest and against migrants and asylum seekers; overcrowding and unhygienic conditions in prisons; societal violence against women, trafficking in persons; and employment discrimination based on sex, gender, disability, and national origin.

The government took steps to prosecute and punish security forces and other officials who committed abuses. Impunity was not widespread.

During the year the country suffered one major terrorist attack, at least three terror-related individual killings targeting police and clergy, and several attempted terrorist attacks that led to investigations and prosecutions. As of the end of the year, police and prosecutors continued to investigate elements of the attacks.

Note: The country includes 11 overseas administrative divisions covered in this report. Four overseas territories in French Guiana, Guadeloupe, Martinique, and La Reunion have the same political status as the 22 metropolitan regions and 101 departments on the mainland. Five divisions are overseas "collectivities": French Polynesia, Saint-Barthelemy, Saint-Martin, Saint-Pierre and Miquelon, and Wallis and Futuna. New Caledonia is a special overseas collectivity with a unique, semiautonomous status between that of an independent country and an overseas department. Citizens of these territories periodically elect deputies and senators to represent them in parliament, like the other overseas regions and departments.

Section 1. Respect for the Integrity of the Person, Including Freedom from:

a. Arbitrary Deprivation of Life and other Unlawful or Politically Motivated Killings

There were no reports the government or its agents committed arbitrary or unlawful killings.

The country suffered several terrorist attacks during the year. On June 13, Larossi Abballa killed a police officer and the officer's partner, a Ministry of Interior civil servant, at their home in Magnanville. On July 14, Mohamed Lahouaiej Bouhlel drove a large truck through a pedestrianized seaside promenade in Nice, killing 86 persons. On July 26, Adel Kermiche and Abdel-Malik Nabil Petitjean attacked a Roman Catholic church in Saint-Quentin-Fallavier, killing a priest and seriously injuring a male worshipper.

b. Disappearance

There were no reports of politically motivated disappearances.

c. Torture and Other Cruel, Inhuman, or Degrading Treatment or Punishment

The constitution and law prohibit such practices, and security and military personnel usually respected human rights principles in their work. There were, however, occasional accusations of abuses.

As of September 15, the defender of rights, the equivalent of an official ombudsman for civil liberties, registered 68 citizen claims of violence committed by security forces.

There were reports police beat, kicked, and used pepper spray on migrants and asylum seekers in the port city of Calais (see section 2.d.).

Credible allegations surfaced during the year that French peacekeepers committed acts of sexual abuse in Sub-Saharan Africa in 2015. These accusations were under investigation by the Ministry of Defense. The allegations emerged in 2015 and included the sexual abuse of homeless children by French troops stationed in the Central African Republic's capital Bangui as part of Operation Sangaris. The Ministry of Defense condemned the alleged abuse. The case was separately under investigation by the Paris prosecutor's office. In February prosecutors widened their probe after two children submitted rape accusations against French soldiers. On April 5, a French judicial source stated that prosecutors opened a third investigation into allegations of sexual abuse by Operation Sangaris troops, which continued at year's end.

Prison and Detention Center Conditions

While prisons and detention centers met many international standards, credible NGOs and government officials reported overcrowding and unhygienic conditions in prisons.

In 2015 the Council of Europe's Committee for the Prevention of Torture (CPT) carried out a periodic visit to the country. The CPT investigated the conditions of deprivation of liberty in three prisons affected by overcrowding and alleged discrepancies in treatment of certain categories of detained and convicted prisoners in different establishments, including in a unit holding "radicalized" prisoners. In addition the CPT carried out a detailed analysis of the involuntary commitment of patients to psychiatric establishments and visited 12 police and gendarmerie stations to examine the material conditions provided for detainees.

In April the UN Committee against Torture considered the report submitted by France. The country corapporteur for France, Alessio Bruni, noted that, despite measures taken by the government, prison overcrowding continued in Marseille, Paris, and Nimes, with the worst detention conditions being in French Polynesia and other overseas territories. He regretted those placed in disciplinary wings and isolation were increasingly at risk of committing suicide, and noted with concern such placement could last up to 30 days. He also criticized the use of isolation in psychiatric hospitals, sometimes for more than 20 hours per day and for periods of up to several months.

Physical Conditions: The maximum acceptable capacity for the country's 191 prisons was 58,507 inmates. As of August the Prison Service reported the country's prisons held 68,819 inmates, representing 118 percent of prison capacity. The number of inmates increased from the end of 2015. Detention conditions for women were often better than for men because overcrowding was less common. The occupancy rate was 223 percent of capacity at the Faa'a Nuutania prison in French Polynesia and 146 percent at the Ducos prison in Martinique.

Although there were no known deaths in prison due to mistreatment or adverse conditions during the year, prison suicides remained a problem. According to the Ministry of Justice, 113 inmates committed suicide in 2015, a rate considerably higher than that outside prison.

On July 19, the administrative court of Caen ordered the state to pay 1,300 euros ($1,430) compensation to an inmate for failing to provide minimum required space in his cell.

In its 2012 report, the CPT raised concerns regarding inadequate medical and psychiatric staffing and degrading treatment of prisoners by prison staff during medical evaluations in some prisons. The CPT report also mentioned detainee complaints of derogatory comments by staff and the lack of opportunities for detainees to work or engage in other activities.

Administration: Authorities investigated credible allegations of inhuman conditions and documented the results in a publicly accessible manner.

Independent Monitoring: The government permitted prison visits by independent human rights observers, both local and foreign. In addition to periodic visits by the

CPT, the UN Committee against Torture regularly examined prisons, most recently in April.

d. Arbitrary Arrest or Detention

The constitution and law prohibit arbitrary arrest and detention, and the government generally observed these prohibitions, although lengthy pretrial detention was a problem.

Role of the Police and Security Apparatus

Under the direction of the Ministry of the Interior, Overseas France, Local Authorities, and Immigration, a civilian national police force of 145,000 and a national gendarmerie of 98,155 maintained internal security. In conjunction with specific gendarmerie units used for military operations, the army was responsible for external security under the Ministry of Defense. Observers considered police and gendarmes generally effective.

Civilian authorities maintained effective control over the national police force, the gendarmerie, and the army, and the government has effective mechanisms to investigate and punish abuse and corruption. Official impunity was not widespread. The inspector general of national police and the Office of Judicial Police investigated and prosecuted allegations of brutality in the police force and the gendarmerie, a unit within the armed forces responsible for general law enforcement. The defender of rights investigated allegations of misconduct by municipal police, gendarmes, and private security forces and reported its findings to the prime minister and parliament. According to the 2015 defender of rights report, individuals filed 910 complaints against security forces in 2015.

In July 2015 the defender of rights called for a ban on police use of flash ball guns during demonstrations following several cases in which demonstrators sustained injuries from the weapon. In 2013 and 2014, the defender of rights was called upon to examine seven cases in which serious injuries or permanent infirmities were allegedly sustained due to the use of flash ball guns. In July 2015 Interior Minister Bernard Cazeneuve announced he would not ban police use of flash-balls. On June 24, in five decisions, the Paris Court of Appeals ordered the government to pay damages to five men who were subjected to unwarranted police identity checks that observers believed constituted racial profiling. The government must pay a 1,500 euro ($1,650) fine to each. The complaints were initially dismissed in a 2013 trial. The plaintiffs claimed they were subjected to unjustified identity checks because of their skin color. The State appealed the ruling.

On November 9, the Supreme Court definitively condemned the government for three unjustified identity checks conducted by police forces.

On September 30, a Caen criminal court sentenced a police officer to a two-month suspended prison sentence for violence committed on May 26 in Caen against a man who was demonstrating against the labor law (see section 2.b.).

Arrest Procedures and Treatment of Detainees

The law requires police to obtain warrants based on sufficient evidence prior to detaining suspects, but police can immediately arrest suspects caught committing an illegal act. Individuals have the right to a judicial notification on the legality of their detention during their first hour in custody, and authorities generally respected this right.

By law police must inform persons taken into custody of their right to remain silent and their right to have a lawyer present during questioning. Authorities must inform detainees of charges against them once they are in police custody, and defense lawyers may ask questions throughout the interrogation. If a medical examination is required, the examiner must respect professional confidentiality. The law forbids complete strip searches except in cases where authorities suspect the accused of hiding dangerous items or drugs. A system of bail exists, and authorities made use of it. Detainees generally had access to a lawyer, and the state provides legal counsel to indigent detainees. The law allows police to detain individuals for up to 24 hours if police suspect them of having committed a crime punishable by a prison sentence. Authorities may extend this period of detention for an additional 24 hours regardless of the seriousness of the crime.

Under the state of emergency in effect during the year, authorities may place persons of interest and their relatives under house arrest if they deem them to pose a threat to national security. As of November 7, authorities had placed 95 persons under house arrest.

In cases involving terrorism or drug trafficking, the law allows extended periods of detention before notification to counsel. Authorities may hold suspects for up to 96 hours without charge or access to a lawyer and may petition a judge to extend detention by an additional 48 hours. Following this maximum six-day period, authorities must either charge suspects or release them.

Pretrial Detention: Long delays in bringing cases to trial and lengthy pretrial detention were problems. Although authorities generally allowed pretrial detention only in cases involving possible sentences of more than three years in prison, some suspects spent many years in detention before trial. As of August pretrial detainees made up approximately 11.5 percent of the prison population.

Detainee's Ability to Challenge Lawfulness of Detention before a Court: Persons arrested or detained, regardless of whether on criminal or other grounds, are entitled to challenge in court the legal basis or arbitrary nature of their detention and obtain prompt release and compensation if found to have been unlawfully detained.

e. Denial of Fair Public Trial

The constitution and law provide for an independent judiciary, and the government generally respected judicial independence, although delays in bringing cases to trial were a problem. The country has no independent military court; rather, the Paris Magistrates Court tries any military personnel alleged to have committed crimes outside the country.

Trial Procedures

The constitution and law provide for the right to a fair trial, and an independent judiciary generally enforced this right. Defendants enjoy a presumption of innocence, and authorities inform defendants of the charges against them at the time of arrest. Except for those involving minors, trials are public and usually held before a judge or tribunal of judges. In cases where the potential punishment exceeds 10 years' imprisonment, a panel of professional and lay judges hears the case. Defendants have the right to be present and to consult with an attorney in a timely manner. Authorities provide an attorney at public expense if needed when defendants face serious criminal charges. Defendants are able to question the testimony of prosecution witnesses and present witnesses and evidence in their defense. Authorities allow defendants adequate time and facilities to prepare a defense. Defendants and their attorneys have access to government-held evidence relevant to their cases. Defendants have the right to remain silent and to appeal.

Political Prisoners and Detainees

There were no reports of political prisoners or detainees.

Civil Judicial Procedures and Remedies

There is an independent and impartial judiciary in civil matters and access to a court to submit lawsuits seeking damages for, or cessation of, human rights violations. Individuals may file complaints with the European Court of Human Rights for alleged violations of the European Convention on Human Rights by the state once they have exhausted avenues for appeal through the domestic courts.

f. Arbitrary or Unlawful Interference with Privacy, Family, Home, or Correspondence

The constitution and law prohibit interference with privacy, family, home, or correspondence, and the government generally respected these prohibitions.

The nationwide state of emergency in effect during the year gives police and prefects authority to search homes without a warrant and authorizes the government to read e-mails and text messages and listen to calls of individuals suspected of having links to terrorist activities. The civil society group La Quadrature du Net expressed concern the state of emergency augmented authorities' ability to carry out invasive searches of homes and seized cell phones. As of November 7, police carried out 4,000 antiterrorism raids across the country under the state of emergency.

The government continued implementing July 2015 amendments to the Interior Security Code that allow specialized intelligence agencies to conduct real-time surveillance without approval from a judge on both networks and individuals for information or documents regarding a person identified as posing a terrorist threat. Since passage of the amendments, the Council of State has issued three implementing decrees designating the agencies that may engage in such surveillance, including using devices to establish geolocation. During the year the Constitutional Council struck down provisions in the code that allowed surveillance of radio communications that was not subject to "any substantive or procedural conditions" as well as the police practice of copying the data on any electronic device during a house search without the consent of the individual or judicial authorization.

Section 2. Respect for Civil Liberties, Including:

a. Freedom of Speech and Press

The constitution and law provide for freedom of speech and press, and the government generally respected these rights. An independent press, an effective judiciary, and a functioning democratic political system combined to provide freedom of speech and press.

Freedom of Speech and Expression: While individuals could criticize the government publicly or privately without reprisal, there were some limitations of freedom of speech. Strict antidefamation laws prohibit racially or religiously motivated verbal and physical abuse. Written or oral speech that incites racial or ethnic hatred and denies the Holocaust or crimes against humanity is illegal. Authorities may deport a noncitizen for publicly using "hate speech" or speech constituting a threat of terrorism.

On September 7, a Paris criminal court pronounced the founding member of the revolutionary group, Action directe, Jean-Marc Rouillan, guilty of condoning terrorism for calling the Bataclan terrorists "really brave." The court sentenced him to eight months in prison.

Press and Media Freedoms: While independent media were active and generally expressed a wide variety of views without restriction, the print and broadcast media, books, and online newspapers and journals were subject to the same antidefamation and hate speech laws that limited freedom of speech.

The law provides protection to journalists, who may be compelled to reveal sources only in cases where serious crimes occurred and access to a journalist's sources was required to complete an official investigation.

Internet Freedom

The government did not restrict or disrupt access to the internet or censor online content, and there were no credible reports that the government monitored private online communications without appropriate legal oversight. According to the International Telecommunication Union, 84.7 percent of the population used the internet in 2015.

The nationwide state of emergency in effect during the year allows blocking of websites and social networks linked to or advocating terrorism and authorizes the government to read emails and text messages of individuals suspected of having links to terrorist activities. As of November 7, authorities blocked 54 websites on these grounds.

In June 2015 the parliament adopted an intelligence bill that granted new powers to the intelligence services to monitor suspected threats to public order and detect future terrorists. The bill also provides an enhanced legal framework for the intelligence services' activities. Civil liberties groups and digital freedom activists opposed the bill and asserted that the rules on intelligence gathering could lead to mass surveillance with inadequate oversight. In July 2015 following its review, the Constitutional Council announced that it approved the majority of the legislation, rejecting only three articles.

According to the law, during a state of emergency exceptional powers allow the interior minister to take "all the measures" necessary to block sites suspected of "condoning terrorism or encouraging acts of terrorism."

On June 3, the country adopted legislation on organized crime and terrorism mandating a maximum sentence of two years' imprisonment and a 30,000 euro ($33,000) fine for consulting terrorist websites. On August 8, a Chartres criminal court sentenced a 31-year-old man to two years in prison for repeatedly visiting and reading websites related to the commission of terrorist acts.

Academic Freedom and Cultural Events

There were no government restrictions on academic freedom or cultural events.

b. Freedom of Peaceful Assembly and Association

Freedom of Assembly

The constitution and law provide for the freedom of assembly, and the government generally respected this right.

The state of emergency in effect during the year grants a number of exceptional powers to authorities, including the right to set curfews, limit the movement of people and forbid mass gatherings, establish secure zones where individuals may be monitored, and close public spaces such as theatres, bars, museums and other meeting places. Prefects in all regions may decide on the provisional closure of concert halls, restaurants, or any public place, and to prohibit public demonstrations or gatherings.

Between March and September, there were 14 demonstrations in the country to protest against the labor law, leading to violent clashes between protesters and police forces. Several demonstrators and unions claimed police used excessive force during the demonstrations. As of June 7, the head of the police internal affairs unit reported that 48 judicial inquiries into police violence had been opened.

Freedom of Association

The constitution and law provide for the freedom of association, and the government generally respected this right.

Under the state of emergency, police and prefects may dissolve associations acting in favor of serious disruption of public order.

c. Freedom of Religion

See the Department of State's *International Religious Freedom Report* at www.state.gov/religiousfreedomreport/.

d. Freedom of Movement, Internally Displaced Persons, Protection of Refugees, and Stateless Persons

The constitution and law provide for freedom of internal movement, foreign travel, emigration, and repatriation, and the government generally respected these rights.

Abuse of Migrants, Refugees, and Stateless Persons: On June 16, the UN Children's Fund (UNICEF) released a study warning that children living in refugee camps such as Calais and Dunkirk were exposed to sexual exploitation, trafficking, and abuse on a daily basis. UNICEF estimated there were approximately 500 unaccompanied children living across seven refugee sites in northern France. It identified cases of debt slavery and forced criminal activity and a "constant threat" of sexual violence. Some young women reported being promised safe passage to the United Kingdom in exchange for sex.

On February 13, seven migrants living in the Calais refugee camp filed lawsuits alleging violent acts committed by police against them between January 21 and February 10. At year's end an investigation into the allegations continued.

The government cooperated with the Office of the UN High Commissioner for Refugees and other humanitarian organizations in providing protection and assistance to refugees, asylum seekers, stateless persons, and other persons of concern.

In October, the government cleared the Calais refugee camp and resettled an estimated 5,600 individuals, including 1,600 unaccompanied minors, in refugee welcome and orientation centers around the country. Migrants had access to basic services, medical care, and information on applying for asylum at these centers. Unaccompanied minors were placed in separate specialized centers that provided additional education and health services for children.

In-country Movement: The law requires persons engaged in itinerant activities with a fixed domicile to obtain a license that is renewable every four years. Itinerant persons without a fixed abode must possess travel documents.

Protection of Refugees

Access to Asylum: The country's laws provide for the granting of asylum or refugee status, and the government has a system for providing protection to refugees. The system was active and accessible to those seeking protection. The Office for the Protection of Refugees and Stateless Refugees (OFPRA) provided asylum application forms in 24 languages, including English, Albanian, Russian, Serbo-Croatian, Turkish, Tamil, and Arabic, although applicants must complete them in French, generally without government language assistance.

In July 2015 the parliament adopted a law on asylum reform to improve procedures for assessing asylum cases. The law requires the reduction of application processing times, from 24 to nine months, and introduces a directed housing system so that asylum seekers are not concentrated in a handful of regions and enjoy better reception conditions.

On September 20, an administrative court ordered the government to pay a 5,500 euro ($6,050) fine to a 16-year-old Iraqi minor of Kurdish origin who was living in the Calais refugee camp after the prefecture did not promptly register his asylum request. The court also found that the prefecture failed to alert the child protection services.

<u>Safe Country of Origin/Transit</u>: The government considered 16 countries to be "safe countries of origin" for purposes of asylum. A "safe country" is one that provides for compliance with the principles of liberty, democracy, rule of law, and fundamental human rights. This policy reduced the chances of an asylum seeker from one of these countries obtaining asylum but did not prevent it. While individuals originating from a safe country of origin may apply for asylum, they may receive only a special form of temporary residence status that allows them to remain in the country. Authorities examined asylum requests through an emergency procedure that may not exceed 15 days. Countries considered "safe" included Albania, Armenia, Benin, Bosnia and Herzegovina, Cabo Verde, Georgia, Ghana, India, Macedonia, Mauritius, Moldova, Mongolia, Montenegro, Senegal, Serbia, and Kosovo.

<u>Refoulement</u>: While the government provided protection against the expulsion or return of persons to countries where their lives or freedom would be threatened, human rights groups regularly criticized its deportation practices for their strict adherence to the law. During the year several French NGOs provided legal advice to migrants and asylum seekers and criticized individual cases of deportations.

<u>Freedom of movement</u>: Authorities maintained administrative holding centers for foreigners who could not be immediately deported. Authorities could hold undocumented migrants in these facilities for a maximum of 45 days. There were 26 holding centers on the mainland and three in the overseas territories with a total capacity of 1,970 persons.

On June 28, five associations (Assfam, Forum-Refugies-Cosi, France Terre d'Asile, Cimade, and Ordre de Malte) providing help to foreigners released a joint annual report on migration for 2015. The report stated that 47,565 undocumented migrants were placed in administrative holding centers in 2015, representing a slight decrease from 2014, when 49,537 were held.

On July 12, the European Court of Human Rights condemned the country for the practice of detaining foreign children in holding centers while their parents were undergoing deportation proceedings. In view of the children's age and the duration and conditions of their administrative detention, the court found that authorities had subjected them to an inhuman and degrading treatment in violation of the European Convention on Human Rights.

<u>Access to Basic Services</u>: In 2013 the defender of rights submitted his report on the overall migration situation in the department of Mayotte, located in the Indian

Ocean. Observing that approximately 3,000 unaccompanied foreign minors on the island were not receiving assistance, the defender of rights sent a letter to the interior minister in 2014 that urged the government to establish a representation of the French Office for Immigration and Integration on Mayotte to provide better support to minors. Since 2012 local police have been allowed to detain suspected undocumented migrants up to four hours for not having a residency permit.

Durable Solutions: The government has provisions to manage a range of solutions for integration, resettlement, and return of migrants and unsuccessful asylum seekers. The government accepted refugees for resettlement from other countries and facilitated local integration and naturalization, particularly of refugees in protracted situations. The government assisted in the safe, voluntary return of migrants and unsuccessful asylum seekers to their home countries. In 2015 the government voluntarily repatriated 4,211 undocumented migrants to their countries of origin.

According to a public statement by President Hollande, since 2011 the country has admitted 10,000 Syrian refugees.

Temporary Protection: Temporary protection is a procedure that provides for immediate temporary protection in the case of a mass influx of migrants and asylum seekers or an imminent influx of displaced persons. Authorities often initiated this protection when the asylum system was unable to process such an influx. Authorities may grant individuals a one-year renewable permit that could be extended for an additional two years. According to OFPRA, the government did not grant temporary protection in 2015.

Stateless Persons

OFPRA reported there were 1,326 stateless persons in the country as of December 2015. It attributed statelessness to various factors, including contradictions among differing national laws, government stripping of nationality, and lack of birth registration. As the agency responsible for the implementation of international conventions on refugees and stateless persons, OFPRA provided benefits to stateless persons. The government provided a one-year residence permit marked "private and family life" to persons deemed stateless that allowed them to work. After two permit renewals, stateless persons could apply for and obtain a 10-year residence permit.

The laws afford individuals the opportunity to gain citizenship. A person may become a citizen if: either parent is a citizen; he or she is legally adopted by a citizen, he or she is born in the country to stateless parents or to individuals whose nationality does not transfer to the child; or he or she marries a citizen. A person who has reached the legal age of majority, 18, may apply for citizenship through naturalization after five years of habitual residence in the country. Applicants for citizenship must have good knowledge of both the French language and civics.

Section 3. Freedom to Participate in the Political Process

The constitution and law provide citizens the ability to choose their government through free and fair periodic elections held by secret ballot and based on universal and equal suffrage.

Elections and Political Participation

Recent Elections: The 2012 presidential and national assembly elections were considered free and fair, as were the 2014 Senate and the December 2015 regional elections.

Participation of Women and Minorities: No laws limit the participation of women and members of minorities in the political process, and they participated actively.

Section 4. Corruption and Lack of Transparency in Government

The law provides criminal penalties for corruption by officials, and the government generally implemented the law effectively. There were some reports of government corruption during the year.

Corruption: On May 4, a Cayenne appeals court sentenced the mayor of Saint-Laurent-du-Maroni in French Guyana to 18 months in prison and a fine of 100,000 euros ($110,000) for complicity in the misappropriation of corporate assets. He was accused of encouraging a private company, whose main shareholder was his municipality, to provide 887,000 euros ($976,000) in compensation benefits to the company's director, a friend and associate of the mayor.

The inspector general of national police and the Inspectorate of the National Gendarmerie actively investigated and prosecuted allegations of police and gendarme corruption. Citizens may report police abuses on the internet through the Ministry of Interior's website, provided they identify themselves. In 2015 citizens registered 2,958 reports online.

Financial Disclosure: The president, members of the parliament and the European Parliament, ministers, regional and departmental council heads, mayors of larger communities, and directors of state-owned companies (post office, railway, and telephone) are required to declare their personal assets to the Commission for the Financial Transparency of Political Life at the beginning and end of their terms. The commission issued and made available to the public periodic reports on officials' financial holdings on a discretionary basis at least once every three years. Officials who fail to comply are subject to sanctions.

The Central Office for Combating Corruption and Financial and Tax Crimes investigates offenses including tax fraud, influence peddling, and failure of elected officials to make financial disclosures or report their own violations of the law.

Public Access to Information: The law provides for public access to government information, and the government provided access for citizens and noncitizens, including foreign media.

Section 5. Governmental Attitude Regarding International and Nongovernmental Investigation of Alleged Violations of Human Rights

A wide variety of domestic and international human rights organizations generally operated, investigated, and published their findings on human rights cases without government restrictions. Government officials were cooperative and responsive to their views.

Government Human Rights Bodies: The National Consultative Commission on Human Rights (CNCDH) advised the government on human rights and produced an annual report on racism and xenophobia. Domestic and international human rights organizations widely considered the CNCDH independent and effective. Observers considered the defender of rights independent and effective, with access to all necessary resources.

Section 6. Discrimination, Societal Abuses, and Trafficking in Persons

Women

<u>Rape and Domestic Violence</u>: The law criminalizes rape, including spousal rape, and domestic violence, and the government generally enforced the law effectively. The penalty for rape is 15 years' imprisonment, which may be increased, depending on the age of the victim and the perpetrator's relationship to the victim. The government and NGOs provided shelters, counseling, and hotlines for rape survivors.

In August 2015 the daily newspaper *Le Figaro* published figures showing that the number of reported rapes in the country increased by 18 percent from 2010 to 2014, while rape allegations involving children rose by more than 20 percent in the same period. Crimes against women who belonged to an ethnic minority were generally underreported, as they were less likely to file a lawsuit if their presence in the country was undocumented.

The law prohibits domestic violence against women and men, including spousal abuse, and the government generally enforced the law. The penalty for domestic violence against either gender varies according to the type of crime, ranging from three years in prison and a fine of 45,000 euros ($49,500) to 20 years in prison. The government reported that spouses killed 115 women and 21 men in domestic violence cases in 2015, a 3.5 percent decrease from 2014. The National Observatory on Delinquency and Criminal Responses estimated that 223,000 women between the ages 18 and 75 residing in the country were victims of physical and sexual domestic violence in metropolitan France in 2010-15. The government sponsored and funded programs targeted at female victims of violence, including shelters, counseling, hotlines, free mobile phones, and a media campaign. The government also supported the work of 25 associations and NGOs dedicated to fighting domestic violence.

The government budgeted 66 million euros ($73 million) to fund its 2014-16 interministerial plan to combat violence against women, a 50 percent increase above the previous three-year plan. The program focused on enhancing protection and social assistance for survivors, increasing the number of social workers in police stations and beds in emergency shelters, lengthening the operating hours of a free emergency domestic abuse hotline, raising public awareness regarding rape and violence against women, and improving training to help health-care and other government employees identify victims.

<u>Female Genital Mutilation/Cutting (FGM/C)</u>: FGM/C is practiced in the country, particularly within diaspora communities where FGM/C was prevalent. The law prohibits FGM/C as "violence involving mutilation or permanent infirmity." It is

punishable by up to 10 years in prison (20 years if it involves a minor under age 15 and when the offense is committed by a person with authority over the minor) and a fine of 150,000 euros ($165,000). The law also criminalizes inciting a minor to undergo FGM/C and inciting another person to perform FGM/C. Both are punishable by up to five years' imprisonment and a fine of up to 75,000 euros ($82,500). The government provides reconstructive surgery and counseling for FGM/C victims.

According to the Ministry of Families, Childhood, and Women's Rights, during 2014 approximately 20,000 women, half of whom were minors, were circumcised or at risk of FGM/C. According to a study released in 2007 by the National Institute for Demographic Studies, 53,000 circumcised women resided in the country. The majority of FGM/C survivors were recent immigrants from sub-Saharan African countries where the procedure was performed.

<u>Sexual Harassment</u>: The law prohibits gender-based harassment of subordinates by superiors. Sexual harassment is defined as "subjecting an individual to repeated acts, comments, or any other conduct of a sexual nature that are detrimental to a person's dignity because of their degrading or humiliating character, thereby creating an intimidating, hostile, or offensive environment." The law divides sexual harassment into two categories: the first, for repeated instances of harassment, carries a maximum sentence of two years' imprisonment and a 30,000 euros ($33,000) fine; the second, for a single serious offense, carries a maximum sentence of three years' imprisonment and a 45,000 euros ($49,500) fine. The law also criminalizes discrimination against transgender individuals.

The Ministry of Justice estimated that 300,000 cases of sexual harassment occurred each year but that only approximately 1,000 victims filed complaints. Of those, approximately 60 resulted in convictions, with an average penalty of 1,000 euros ($1,100). In 2014 the defender of rights published a French Institute of Public Opinion survey that indicated one in five women reported facing sexual harassment in her professional life and that 5 percent of those cases were brought to trial. According to a report released by parliament on November 16, a total of 1,048 lawsuits were filed in 2014, of which 65 led to convictions, representing a 6.2 percent conviction rate.

In 2014 Defense Minister Le Drian announced an action plan to fight sexual harassment and violence against women in the armed forces. The plan focused on four main areas: victims' assistance, prevention, transparency (notably the publication of annual statistics on this matter), and disciplinary sanctions. The plan also included the creation of a surveillance unit to protect victims of sexual harassment and violence in the army.

In July 2015 Minister of State for Women's Rights Boistard, Interior Minister Cazeneuve, and Transport Minister Vidalies announced a 12-point plan to combat sexual harassment on public transport, including a text alert system to report incidents more rapidly. The announcement followed a survey, published in April 2015 by the High Council for Equality between Men and Women, in which 100 percent of 600 women surveyed from Seine-Saint-Denis and Essonne reported they had experienced sexual harassment on public transport.

Reproductive Rights: Couples and individuals have the right to decide the number, spacing, and timing of their children, manage their reproductive health, and had the information and means to do so, free from discrimination, coercion, and violence.

Discrimination: The law prohibits gender-based job discrimination and harassment of subordinates by superiors but does not apply to relationships between peers. The constitution and law provide for the same legal status and rights for women as for men, including under family, religious, personal status, labor, property, nationality, and inheritance laws. The Ministry for Families, Childhood and Women's Rights is responsible for protecting the legal rights of women. The constitution and law provide for equal access to professional and social positions and the government generally enforced the laws.

There was discrimination against women with respect to employment and occupation (see section 7.d.) and women were underrepresented in most levels of government leadership.

Children

Birth Registration: The law confers nationality to a child born to at least one parent with citizenship or to a child born in the country to stateless parents or to parents whose nationality does not transfer to the child. Parents must register births of children regardless of citizenship within three days at the local city hall. Parents who do not register within this period are subject to legal action.

Early and Forced Marriage: The minimum legal age for marriage is 18. Child marriage was a problem, particularly in communities of African or Asian descent. According to human rights observers, 70,000 children between ages 10 and 18 were at risk of forced marriage. Although most forced marriage ceremonies occurred outside the country, authorities took steps to address the problem. The law provides for the prosecution of forced marriage cases, even when the marriage occurred abroad. Penalties for violations are up to three years' imprisonment and a 45,000 euro ($49,500) fine. Women and girls could seek refuge at shelters if their parents or guardians threatened them with forced marriage. The government offered educational programs to inform young women of their rights.

<u>Female Genital Mutilation/Cutting (FGM/C)</u>: See information regarding girls under age 18 in the women's section above.

<u>Sexual Exploitation of Children</u>: The law criminalizes the statutory rape of minors under age 15, the minimum age for consensual sex, and the government generally enforced the law effectively. The penalty for statutory rape is 15 years' imprisonment, which may be increased depending on the age of the victim and relationship to the accused. The law criminalizes the commercial sexual exploitation of children. The penalty for sexual exploitation of children is 10 years' imprisonment and a fine of 1,500,000 euros ($1,650,000). If the minor is under age 15, the penalty is increased to 15 years' imprisonment and a 3,000,000-euro ($3.3 million) fine. The sale or trafficking of children is punishable by 10 years' imprisonment and a 1,500,000 euro ($1,650,000) fine. The government and NGOs provided shelters, counseling, and hotlines for statutory rape survivors. The law prohibits child pornography, and the maximum penalty for its use and distribution is five years' imprisonment and a 75,000 euro ($82,500) fine.

According to the most recent estimate available, a 2007 parliamentary report by the Commission on Foreign Affairs, between 3,000 and 8,000 children were sexually exploited in the country each year. Unaccompanied foreign minors were exploited for sexual purposes. Reports indicated that significant numbers of children, primarily from Romania, West Africa, and North Africa, were victims of forced prostitution in the country.

On June 16, a UNICEF study warned that children living in refugee camps such as Calais and Dunkirk were exposed to sexual exploitation, trafficking, and abuse on a daily basis (see section 2.d., Abuse of Migrants, Refugees, and Stateless Persons).

<u>International Child Abductions</u>: The country is a party to the 1980 Hague Convention on the Civil Aspects of International Child Abduction. See the Department of State's *Annual Report on International Parental Child Abduction* at <u>travel.state.gov/content/childabduction/english/legal/compliance.html</u>.

Anti-Semitism

There were approximately 550,000 Jewish residents in the country.

NGO and government observers reported numerous anti-Semitic incidents during the year, including physical and verbal assaults and attacks on synagogues, cemeteries, and memorials. On December 2, former interior minister Cazeneuve announced a significant decrease in anti-Semitic acts committed between January 1 and October 31. The statistics, based on complaints filed with police and gendarmes, showed the number of anti-Semitic acts (including threats and attacks) dropped by 61 percent compared with the same period in 2015.

Both the Ministry of Interior and the Jewish Community Protection Service's annual report cited 808 anti-Semitic incidents in 2015, compared with 851 in 2014. Although they made up only one percent of the country's population, Jews were the target of approximately 40 percent of hate crimes. According to press reports, anti-Semitism was causing a growing number of French Jews to leave their suburban homes and move to Paris. The mayor of Sarcelles, a Paris suburb, reportedly stated that he became aware of "a phenomenon of internal migration" approximately five or six years earlier and claimed that it was getting worse.

On January 11, a 15-year-old Turkish teenager of Kurdish origin stabbed a 35-year-old Jewish teacher with a machete in the southern city of Marseille. The attack took place as the teacher, who was wearing a yarmulke, was on his way to work at the Franco-Hebraic institute. The assailant injured the teacher slightly before being stopped and arrested by the police 10 minutes later. On January 13, the teenager was formally charged with "attempted murder on the grounds of religion and terrorist sympathizing" and placed in pretrial detention.

During the year the French cartoonist Zeon, who had a reputation for anti-Semitic and anti-Israel artwork, won the second International Holocaust Cartoon Contest sponsored by the Iranian newspaper *Hamshahri* in Tehran. His cartoon depicted the entry gate of a Nazi death camp atop a cash register with "six million" in cash inside. The National Bureau for the Vigilance against Anti-Semitism filed a lawsuit against Zeon for displaying anti-Semitic posters in various places around in Paris in 2011. On November 10, he appeared before the Paris criminal court.

President Hollande and other government leaders condemned anti-Semitism during the year.

In January 2015 Amedy Coulibaly killed four Jewish hostages and critically injured four others at a supermarket in Paris before being killed by police. As of January, seven men had been formally charged and placed in pretrial detention for their alleged links to Coulibaly. According to the Ministry of Interior, as of January, 12,000 sites were protected by security forces across the country, 26 percent of them Jewish.

In March the mayor of Montpellier, Philippe Saurel, joined Mayors United against Anti-Semitism, an initiative calling on municipal leaders to publicly address and take concrete actions against anti-Semitism. Other participating cities included Paris, Toulouse, Strasbourg, Bordeaux, Nice, and Nancy.

Trafficking in Persons

See the Department of State's *Trafficking in Persons Report* at www.state.gov/j/tip/rls/tiprpt/.

Persons with Disabilities

The constitution and law prohibit discrimination against persons with physical, sensory, intellectual, and mental disabilities in employment, education, air travel and other transportation, access to health care, and the provision of other government services. The government generally enforced these provisions effectively.

While the law requires companies with more than 20 workers to hire persons with disabilities, many such companies failed to do so (see section 7.d.).

The law requires that buildings, education, and employment be accessible to persons with disabilities. According to government estimates, 40 percent of establishments in the country were accessible. In July 2015 the parliament ratified decrees that extend the deadline for owners to make their buildings and facilities accessible by three to nine years. On May 20, President Hollande announced that, as of May 1, a half million public buildings across the country were undergoing major renovation work to improve accessibility.

In 2013 the Council of Europe issued a resolution that criticized the country for not fulfilling its educational obligations to persons with autism. The council's European Committee of Social Rights concluded that the country was violating the

European Social Charter and called on it to report on its progress in improving the schooling of children and training of young adults with autism. According to NGOs, only 20 percent of the estimated 80,000-100,000 children with autism in the country attended school; the government meanwhile estimated that 29,000 children with autism attended school during the 2015-16 school year.

In April a Strasbourg administrative court ordered the government to pay a 3,800 euros ($4,200) fine to the family of a young boy with a disability for failing to facilitate his education.

The law requires the establishment of centers in each administrative department to help individuals with disabilities in receiving compensation and employment assistance. During the year one million persons with disabilities received financial support from the government. As of September the government paid each adult with disabilities 808.46 euros ($890) per month.

In April 2015 the minister of state for persons with disabilities and the fight against exclusion announced the enhancement of the government's autism plan for 2013-17. On May 20, President Hollande announced that 60 separate classes in preschool and kindergarten for children with autism had been created since 2012.

National/Racial/Ethnic Minorities

Societal violence and discrimination against immigrants of North African origin, Roma, and other ethnic minorities remained a problem. Many observers expressed concern that discriminatory hiring practices in both the public and private sectors deprived minorities from sub-Saharan Africa, the Maghreb, the Middle East, and Asia of equal access to employment.

Citizens, asylum seekers, and migrants may report cases of discrimination based on national origin and ethnicity to the defender of rights. According to the most recent data available, in 2015 the defender of right's office received 4,846 discrimination claims, 22.6 percent of which concerned discrimination based on ethnic origin.

In one prominent case from 2013, the National Front party suspended a local electoral candidate, Anne-Sophie Leclere, for a Facebook posting indicating she would prefer to see then justice minister Christiane Taubira, who was black, "swinging from the branches rather than in government." In 2014 the criminal court in Cayenne, French Guiana, sentenced Leclere to nine months in prison, banned her from holding public office for five years, and fined her 50,000 euros ($55,000). The court also fined the National Front 30,000 euro ($33,000). Both parties appealed the ruling. In June 2015 the Cayenne appeals court cancelled the nine-month prison sentence. The court also ruled that the legal action against Leclere, filed by the Guyanese association Walwari, was not admissible. On September 28, the Paris criminal court sentenced her to a suspended 3,000 euros ($3,300) fine.

Based on unofficial government estimates, the Muslim community was between five and six million persons and consisted primarily of immigrants from former French North African and sub-Saharan colonies and their descendants. Government observers and NGOs reported a number of anti-Muslim incidents during the year, including slurs against Muslims, attacks on mosques, and physical assaults. The National Islamophobia Observatory of the French Council of the Muslim Faith, citing Interior Ministry figures, registered a 63 and 79 percent decrease in anti-Muslim racist incidents and threats during the first half of the year compared with the same period in 2015.

The National Islamophobia Observatory of the French Council of the Muslim Faith, citing Interior Ministry figures, registered a 52 percent decrease in anti-Muslim racist acts during the first 10 months of the year compared with the same period in 2015. From January 1 to September 30, 149 anti-Muslim acts were committed compared to 323 during the same period in 2015.

Following a December 2015 demonstration against an ambush on that injured two firefighters in a housing project in Ajaccio, Corsica, a mob attacked a Muslim prayer room and tried to set fire to copies of the Quran. The mob also vandalized a kebab shop and shouted slogans, such as "Arabs get out!" and "This is our home!" in the Corsican language. Corsican nationalist leaders condemned both incidents as racist acts. Interior Minister Cazeneuve condemned the acts as "intolerable" acts against a place of worship that carried the "odor of racism and xenophobia." Corsica's prefect, Christophe Mirmand, announced that he would ban protests in and around the Jardins de l'Empereur estate after riot police and gendarmes stopped a crowd of approximately 300 persons from entering it. In December 2015 two men were formally charged for links to the attack on firefighters; a date for their trial had not been set by year's end.

On April 30, a Muslim prayer hall in Corsica was destroyed by a fire. According to Ajaccio's public prosecutor, based on hydrocarbon traces found inside the hall the fire was probably a criminal act. No one was injured in the fire. The same day

President Hollande issued a statement expressing his solidarity with the Muslims of Corsica. An investigation into the incident continued at year's end.

In an August 26 decision, the country's highest administrative court, the Council of State, rejected the city of Villeneuve-Loubet's ban on conservative, full-body swimwear worn by some Muslim women. Municipalities claimed the ban was put in place as a security measure following the July attacks in Nice. In its ruling the court asserted the beachwear posed no real risk to public order and, in the absence of such risk, the restriction of individual freedoms could not be justified. The mayors of several cities including Nice dismissed the verdict and announced they would continue to enforce bans on full-body swimwear at public beaches.

Societal hostility against Roma, including Romani migrants from Romania and Bulgaria, continued to be a problem. There were reports of anti-Roma violence by private citizens. Romani individuals, including migrants, experienced discrimination in employment (see section 7.d.). According to a government study, an estimated 20,000 Roma resided in the country.

Authorities dismantled camps and makeshift homes inhabited by Roma throughout the year. In the first half of the year, the European Roma Rights Center (ERRC) reported the eviction of 4,615 Roma in 37 different localities. According to ERRC and Human Rights League data, authorities evicted 11,128 Roma from 111 illegal camps in 2015, an 18 percent decrease from 2014, when 13,483 Roma were evicted. According to the ERRC, of the 111 settlement evictions, 76 followed a court decision and 31 followed a municipal or prefect order. Given the lack of housing alternatives, individuals generally moved to other camps after their eviction. In its annual report covering 2015, Amnesty International reported that authorities conducted forced evictions of Roma and failed to provide adequate alternative housing to evicted Romani individuals and families.

In September 2015 the UN High Commissioner for Human Rights Zeid Ra'ad al-Hussein expressed serious concern regarding forced evictions of Roma and Travelers in the country. He warned that authorities appeared to be making such evictions "systematic national policy" since 2012, noting the August 2015 eviction of more than 150 inhabitants of a shantytown in the Paris suburb of La Courneuve. Al Hussein noted that failure to improve treatment of Roma "simply exacerbates entrenched popular discrimination against what is already one of Europe's most deprived and marginalized communities." He also noted that during the year both the UN Committee for the Elimination of Racial Discrimination and the Human

Rights Committee asked authorities to refrain from forced evictions if they did not provide alternative housing.

On May 2, the French National Consultative Commission on Human Rights noted in its annual report that persistent societal tensions regarding the acceptance of certain minorities, notably the Romani population, and emphasized that anti-Roma prejudice remained high. In June the Operational Platform for Roma Equality, a network of European agencies, stated that evictions had a particularly traumatizing impact on children, leaving them vulnerable to trafficking and other abuses.

In August a group of unknown assailants attacked Roma living in a Marseille settlement with a knife and a Molotov cocktail. Seven persons were hospitalized, according to local media. At year's end no suspects had been arrested in the case.

On September 27, the Collective for the Right of Roma Children to Education released a study conducted between November 2015 and July in 34 shantytowns across the country showing that 53 percent of children between ages 12 and 18 were not attending school.

Regarding "gens du voyage" (or Travelers), the law requires municipalities with more than 5,000 inhabitants to provide a campsite for Travelers with sanitary facilities and access to water and electricity. According to authorities, the law is meant to accommodate Travelers by preventing them from parking on unauthorized sites. As of 2010 the most recent year for which data were available, municipalities had built only 52 percent of the campsites required by law.

The government attempted to combat racism and discrimination through programs that promoted public awareness and brought together local officials, police, and citizens. Some public school systems also managed antidiscrimination education programs. In September 2015 the Ministry of Justice launched a website to inform and assist victims of discrimination.

On April 18, Labor Minister Myriam El Khomri, Economy Minister Emmanuel Macron, Youth Minister Patrick Kanner, and State Secretary for Real Equality Ericka Bareigts jointly inaugurated a national campaign to counter hiring discrimination. Labor Minister El Khomri announced that blind resume testing would be used to name and shame companies found guilty of biases in hiring.

On May 9, the ombudsman for human rights, Jacques Toubon, released a report on government discrimination against foreigners and failure to uphold their fundamental rights. The report noted several examples, including retired workers from Benin who could not get a state pension because they did not have French citizenship, despite having worked in the country for most their lives, and schools that refused to accept children of irregular migrants, despite being required to do so by law. The report called on the government to "prevent the spread of divergent or illegal interpretations of the law" in order to protect foreigners living in the country.

Acts of Violence, Discrimination, and Other Abuses Based on Sexual Orientation and Gender Identity

The law prohibits discrimination based on sexual orientation and gender identity. The statute of limitations is 12 months for offenses related to sex, sexual orientation, gender identity, and disability. Authorities pursued and punished perpetrators of violence based on sexual orientation or gender identity.

The NGO SOS Homophobia reported 1,318 homophobic acts in 2015, a 40 percent decrease from 2014. It reported 152 instances of physical assault, a 6 percent decrease from 2014.

On October 12, the parliament adopted a legal gender recognition procedure that removed requirements for individuals to undergo sterilization and provide proof of medical treatment in order to confirm their gender recognition. Human rights organizations welcomed this development but criticized the government for still requiring individuals to undergo a judicial process to change the legal documentation of their gender.

Section 7. Worker Rights

a. Freedom of Association and the Right to Collective Bargaining

The constitution and labor law provide workers, including migrant workers, the right to form and join unions of their choice without previous authorization or excessive requirements. The law provides for the right to bargain collectively and allows unions to conduct their activities without interference. Workers, except those in certain essential services such as police and the armed forces, have the right to strike unless the strike threatens public safety. The law prohibits antiunion discrimination and forbids removing a candidate from a recruitment procedure for asking about union membership or trade union activities. The Ministry of Labor, Employment, Vocational Training, and Social Dialogue enforces related regulations and provides penalties in cases of discrimination of up to three years' imprisonment and a 45,000 euro ($59,500) fine. These penalties proved generally sufficient to deter violations.

Public-sector workers must declare their intention to strike at least 48 hours before the strike commences. Furthermore, a notification of intention to strike is permissible only after negotiations between trade unions and employers have broken down. Workers are not entitled to receive pay while striking. Wages, however, may be paid retroactively. For road transportation strikes, the law on minimum service provides for wages to be calculated proportionally to time worked while striking. Health-care workers are required to provide a minimum level of service during strikes. Laws in the rail and passenger transport sectors prescribe minimum service levels that public transport workers must maintain during a strike; transport users must also receive clear and reliable information on the services that would run in the event of a disruption. Authorities effectively enforced laws and regulations prohibiting retaliation against strikers.

Workers freely exercised their rights to form and join unions, conduct union activities, and bargain collectively. Workers' organizations stressed their independence vis-a-vis political parties. Some of their leaders, however, did not conceal their political affiliations. Although the law prohibits antiunion discrimination, union representatives noted that it occasionally occurred, particularly in small companies. The government and employers respected freedom of association and the right to collective bargaining.

b. Prohibition of Forced or Compulsory Labor

The law prohibits all forms of forced or compulsory labor. The law recognizes the offenses of forced labor and forced servitude as crimes and provides for imprisonment of up to seven and 10 years, respectively, as punishment for violations. These fines generally proved sufficient to deter violations.

Men, women, and children, mainly from Eastern Europe, West Africa, and Asia, were subject to forced labor, including domestic servitude (also see section 7.c.). There were no government estimates on the extent of forced labor among domestic workers, many of whom were migrant women and children. In 2015 the NGO Committee against Modern Slavery assisted 145 victims of forced labor, the majority of whom were women employed in domestic work. The government attempted to address forced labor by providing financial assistance to NGOs who are responsible for providing assistance to victims.

On March 22, a criminal court in Nancy sentenced a couple to a two-year suspended prison sentence for exploiting a young Algerian girl over a period of seven years. The couple was also sentenced to pay a fine of 6,000 euros ($6,600) each to the victim.

Also see the Department of State's *Trafficking in Persons Report* at www.state.gov/j/tip/rls/tiprpt/.

c. Prohibition of Child Labor and Minimum Age for Employment

The minimum age for employment is 16. There are exceptions for persons enrolled in certain apprenticeship programs or working in the entertainment industry, who are subject to further labor regulations for minors. The law generally prohibits persons under age 18 from performing work considered arduous or dangerous such as working with dangerous chemicals, high temperatures, heavy machinery, electrical wiring, metallurgy, dangerous animals, working at heights, or work that exposes minors to acts or representations of a pornographic or violent nature. It is also prohibited for persons under age 18 to work on Sunday, or between 10 p.m. and 6 a.m.

The government effectively enforced labor laws, although some children were exploited in the worst forms of child labor, including commercial sexual exploitation and forced criminal activity. Inspectors from the Ministry of Labor, Employment, Vocational Training, and Social Dialogue investigated workplaces to enforce compliance with all labor statutes. To prohibit violations of child labor statutes, inspectors may place employers under observation or refer them for criminal prosecution. Employers convicted of using child labor risk up to five years' imprisonment and a 75,000 euro ($82,500) fine. These penalties proved generally sufficient to deter violations. According to the report of the Court of Audit released during the year, there were 2,462 inspectors and comptrollers.

There were reports of Romani children engaged in forced begging, and some migrant children were in situations of domestic servitude. Commercial sexual exploitation of children also occurred (see section 6, Children).

d. Discrimination with Respect to Employment and Occupation

The labor code prohibits discrimination based upon an individual's national origin, religion, race, sex, lifestyle, sexual orientation, age, family situation, pregnancy, state of health or disability, economic situation and place of residence. Authorities generally enforced this prohibition.

A gender equality law provides measures to reinforce equality in the workplace as well as sanctions against companies whose noncompliance could prevent women from bidding for public contracts. The law also requires employers to conduct yearly negotiations with employees on professional and pay equity between women and men in companies with more than 50 employees.

Employment discrimination on the basis of sex, gender, disability, and national origin occurred.

The law requires that women receive equal pay for equal work. In a study released during the year, the National Institute of Statistics and Economic Studies found in 2013, the most recent year for which data were available, the average annual private sector salary was 23,140 euros ($25,500) for men. Women on average earned 17,460 euros ($19,200) or 75 percent of the average salary for men. Salary depended on qualifications, age, and sex. The same study in 2016 also indicated 18 percent of salaried men in the private sector held managerial positions, while 13 percent of women with similar skills were managers. Low-skilled jobs were occupied mainly by women. Some 63 percent of nonqualified workers are women. Women were generally much more likely to work part time, due in part to child-care responsibilities: 15.7 percent of women worked part time, compared with 9.2 percent of men.

According to a 2014 survey on gender equality by the defender of rights, pregnant women were most vulnerable to workplace discrimination, with 80 percent of those surveyed reporting workplace discrimination due to pregnancy. One-third of those surveyed reported they witnessed discrimination after a woman returned to work from maternity leave.

The Fund Management Organization for the Professional Integration of People with Disabilities (AGEFIPH) reported the unemployment rate for persons with disabilities grew 25 percent in 2015, faster than the growth rate for the general population (10 percent). The law requires at least 6 percent of the workforce in companies with more than 20 employees be persons with disabilities. The law requires noncompliant companies to contribute to a fund managed by AGEFIPH. Approximately 52 percent of companies met the requirement in 2013; 48 percent contributed into the fund, while a small number (mostly large corporations) received an exemption from the government based on a negotiated action plan, according to AGEFIPH.

As of January 2014, the country lifted work restrictions for Romanian and Bulgarian citizens. Access by Romani migrants to the country's labor market, however, did not improve their living conditions due to the country's high unemployment rate, the lack of requisite professional skills and experience among many Roma, and employer reluctance to hire them.

e. Acceptable Conditions of Work

During the year the government raised the national gross minimum wage to 9.67 euros ($10.60) per hour, effective January 1. The Ministry of Labor enforced the minimum wage. According to 2014 data, the most recent year for which it was available, the poverty-level income rate was 1,008 euros ($1,110) per month for an individual, 1,512 euros ($1,660) for a couple, and 2,116 euros ($2,330) for a couple with two children under age 14.

The official workweek is 35 hours, although companies may negotiate exceptions with employees. The maximum number of working days for workers is 235 days per year. Maximum hours of work are set at 10 hours per day, 48 hours per week, and an average of 44 hours per week during a 12-week work period. Workdays and overtime hours are fixed by a convention or an agreement in each sector in accordance with the labor code.

Employees are entitled to a daily rest period of at least 11 hours and a weekly break of at least 24 hours total, not including the daily rest period. Employers are required to give workers a 20-minute break during a six-hour workday. Premium pay of 25 percent is mandatory for overtime and work on weekends and holidays. The standard amount of paid leave is five weeks per year (2.5 weekdays per month, equivalent to 30 weekdays per year). Some companies also allowed other compensatory days for work in excess of 35 hours to 39 hours per week, called "spare-time account" (RTT). Work in excess of 39 hours per week generally was remunerated.

The government sets occupational health and safety standards in addition to those set by the EU. Government standards cover all employees and sectors. Individual workers could report work hazards to labor inspectors, unions, or (for companies with more than 50 employees) their company health committee, but they did not have an explicit right to remove themselves from a hazardous workplace.

The Ministry of Labor, Employment, Vocational Training, and Social Dialogue is responsible for enforcing the law governing conditions of work and did so effectively in both the formal and informal economy. The government permitted salaries below the minimum wage for certain categories of employment, such as subsidized jobs and internships, that must conform to separate, clearly defined standards. Labor inspectors enforced compliance with the labor law. Disciplinary sanctions at work are strictly governed by the labor code to protect employees from abuse of power by their employers. Employees could pursue appeals in a special labor court up to the Court of Cassation. Sanctions depend on the loss sustained by the victim and were usually applied on a case-by-case basis.

Penalties for labor violations depend on the status of the accused. The law provides for employers and physical persons convicted of labor violations to be imprisoned for up to three years and to pay fines of up to 45,000 euros ($49,500) with additional penalties, including the prohibition to conduct a commercial or industrial enterprise. The law provides for legal persons found guilty of labor violations to be fined up to 225,000 euros ($248,000) and face additional sanctions, such as closing the establishment, placing it under judicial supervision, making the judgment public, confiscating equipment, or dissolving the establishment as a legal person.

Employers, except those in the informal economy, generally adhered to the minimum wage requirement. Immigrants were more likely to face hazardous work, generally because of their concentration in sectors such as agriculture, construction, and hospitality services.